WHISPERS
in the
WILDERNESS

Whispers
in the
Wilderness

Erik Stensland

Morning Light Photography
P.O. Box 2843
Estes Park, CO 80517
www.ImagesofRMNP.com & www.MorningLight.us

All photos and text by Erik Stensland, ImagesofRMNP.com

Book design by Jerry Dorris, AuthorSupport.com
Edited by Janna Nysewander

Special thanks to reviewers: Joanna Stensland, Carl Schmidt, Nancy Conley, Shawn Wignall, Bob Chase, Derek Brooks, John Cooksey, and Sarah Deziel.

ISBN: 978-0-9969626-6-7

Printed in South Korea

Front cover: North Inlet Trail, Rocky Mountain National Park

To those who give themselves
for the preservation of wilderness.

The deep, meaningful, and true things don't shout, they whisper.
Though they run through the heart of all things, they are only
perceived by those who have learned to embrace the silence.

CONTENTS

INTRODUCTION

The history of humankind is inseparably intertwined with the natural world. Until the Industrial Revolution, our lives were deeply influenced by our relationship to the earth. We lived by its seasons, we gathered our food from its fields and forests, we collected our water from the running streams and rivers, and we lay down to sleep beneath the starry sky. We weren't always in such a hurry. We were able to sit and listen to the sound of the wind, watch the flight of a hawk, or witness a mother deer care for her young. We knew the world in a deep and intimate way, recognizing our dependence upon it and seeing ourselves in relation to it. These days the natural world is something foreign. We've built a human society that is almost completely separate from nature, an artificial world designed to insulate and protect us from it. We've created our own isolated sphere of hurry and stress. One of the paradoxical and yet deeply connected results of that separation is that we've also become increasingly disconnected from our own inner lives. We are too busy and outwardly focused to recognize what is happening deep within. Through these pages I'd like to rekindle something of that contemplative connection with the earth and with our inner selves.

In my previous writings I focused on the factual components of the natural world, trying to bring a greater understanding of this domain from which we are so separated. In this book I take a much more reflective approach. Here, my aim is not to explain nature, but to explore our inner lives through the window of the natural world. As I do this, I want to be clear that I believe mountains, trees, elk, and pika do not exist for our benefit. They exist in their own right and aren't here for the purpose of giving us moral lessons, yet there is so much we can learn from them. I believe nature can serve as a mirror, enabling us to see ourselves and our situations with greater clarity.

Most of this book was first written on a trail somewhere in Rocky Mountain National Park as I hiked to or from a photography location. Many of the longer hikes give me a chance to reflect on life and what is happening deep inside of me. These thoughts became the foundation of this book, and I think you will find in the quietness that your inner life isn't all that different from my own. Within each of us are depths we rarely explore. We tend to stay where it seems safe, on the shallow edges. My heartfelt hope is that this book will encourage you to fearlessly head out into the deep water, for there you will find riches of which few are even aware. Out there, beyond our comfort zone, awaits a life of deep peace, security, and greater joy than many of us know is possible.

This book is meant to be read in small bites that are savored and slowly digested, as each page stands on its own. I'd recommend that you read no more than a page or two a day. If you sit down and read it quickly, you will miss most of what I'm trying to communicate. My hope is that you will take the time to plunge beneath my words and images to reflect on the words spoken in your own inner being, for those words are vastly more important than the ones I have written.

*Between every two pine trees there is a
door leading to a new way of life.*

— JOHN MUIR

WILD EMBRACE

"Slow down and breathe deeply," I tell myself as I struggle to take in enough air. For the last four hours I've been hiking as fast as my body will carry me, first along well-worn paths, then through the middle of dark woods alongside a lonely stream, followed by a scramble up to a ridgeline above the trees. Finally I begin to feel like I have escaped—escaped from the eyes of people and their many expectations.

Above me clouds gently float past, leisurely crossing over the mountaintops without seeming to notice them. Down below me there is a large forested valley, free of trail or any obvious sign of human touch. I'm finally all alone, embraced by this mountain wilderness. As my cares fade and my body relaxes, I realize within me a deep sense of belonging. In my bones I can feel this is where I belong, or at least where I long to be.

How can this place, in some ways so inhospitable to people, seem to speak words of belonging to my deepest self? Have we cut ourselves off from the world to which we truly belong? Is the wilderness reminding me of some prehistoric relationship between humanity and nature, or is it the silence of this place that is inviting me to reunite with my inner self and with the whisper on the wind? Perhaps it is both of these and more. In this solitary place I can almost hear the wilderness whispering to each of us to come and be reconnected with nature and with ourselves.

RESTORATION AREA

If you spend any time hiking around the front country of Rocky Mountain National Park, you will regularly find signs like these saying, Restoration Area—Stay Off. These are placed in areas that have been heavily visited, where the feet of far too many people have worn down the grass and flowers to bare dirt, turning a place of lush beauty into an area that resembles a well-used football field.

My life is often like those areas. The day-to-day stress and busyness have me running over the sacred ground in my life, thoughtlessly trampling those delicate places. I become worn and hardened as I focus on efficiency rather than beauty, on productivity rather than meaning. Our modern life is one of incessant activity, which leaves us breathless and harried. We race from meeting to meeting and one responsibility to another. There is so much to do that we never have time to stop. We live by the old idiom, "Don't let the grass grow under your feet" without realizing we are killing any green and hopeful thing in our life.

Yet I find great hope in these restoration signs. After years of watching them, I've seen these places spring back to life when they are given the space they deserve. What looked to be a hopeless situation was simply a garden waiting for the opportunity to thrive. All it took was for someone to draw a boundary and declare this area off limits, once again giving it the space to grow.

THE CAVE

In late August as I hiked through one of the most remote locations in Rocky Mountain National Park, I came across a large cave that had been created by fallen rock from the slopes high above. From a distance, I tried to peer into the cave, but it was dark and intimidating. I was sure a bear or other large animal must have taken up residence in this ideal shelter, so I quickly moved on. A couple of hours later, as I made my way through this area again, a powerful storm appeared over the high peaks. The clouds were black and the temperature had dropped to near freezing. Soon I was surrounded by intense lightning and rain. It was clear I would soon be soaked to the bone, so I ran toward the place where I had seen the cave. After quickly checking to see that there wasn't a pile of fresh bones at the cave entrance, I ventured within this forbidding place. Instead of the angry predator I had feared, I found a peaceful refuge from the storm.

I often think our inner lives are a lot like this cave. We glance into the darkness and quickly step backward. It is an unknown and unsettling place we want to avoid. We wonder what monsters might lurk within just beyond our sight. Could there be some horrible revelation about ourselves in there, or even a darkness that will consume us? It is tempting to stay at the edge, yet something seems to beckon us to enter and face what is inside.

It takes a lot of courage to take that first step, yet once you begin to enter, you'll find it's not as scary as it first looked. As you journey inward you'll realize there is a voice beckoning you to head deeper and deeper within. It is the voice of Wholeness calling out to you.

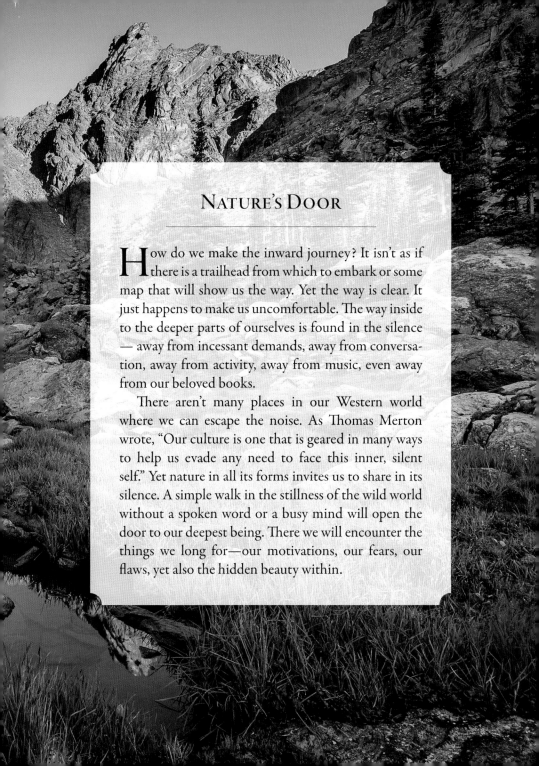

NATURE'S DOOR

How do we make the inward journey? It isn't as if there is a trailhead from which to embark or some map that will show us the way. Yet the way is clear. It just happens to make us uncomfortable. The way inside to the deeper parts of ourselves is found in the silence — away from incessant demands, away from conversation, away from activity, away from music, even away from our beloved books.

There aren't many places in our Western world where we can escape the noise. As Thomas Merton wrote, "Our culture is one that is geared in many ways to help us evade any need to face this inner, silent self." Yet nature in all its forms invites us to share in its silence. A simple walk in the stillness of the wild world without a spoken word or a busy mind will open the door to our deepest being. There we will encounter the things we long for—our motivations, our fears, our flaws, yet also the hidden beauty within.

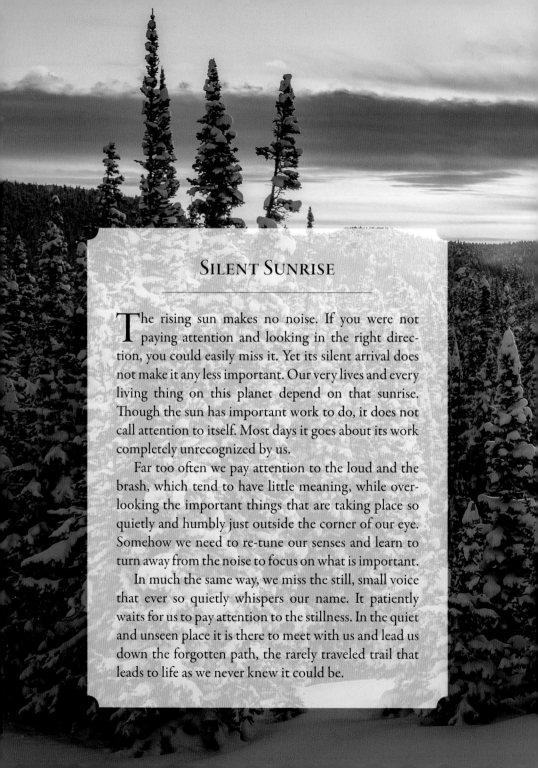

Silent Sunrise

The rising sun makes no noise. If you were not paying attention and looking in the right direction, you could easily miss it. Yet its silent arrival does not make it any less important. Our very lives and every living thing on this planet depend on that sunrise. Though the sun has important work to do, it does not call attention to itself. Most days it goes about its work completely unrecognized by us.

Far too often we pay attention to the loud and the brash, which tend to have little meaning, while overlooking the important things that are taking place so quietly and humbly just outside the corner of our eye. Somehow we need to re-tune our senses and learn to turn away from the noise to focus on what is important.

In much the same way, we miss the still, small voice that ever so quietly whispers our name. It patiently waits for us to pay attention to the stillness. In the quiet and unseen place it is there to meet with us and lead us down the forgotten path, the rarely traveled trail that leads to life as we never knew it could be.

Re-tune

It is not uncommon for our first experiences with silence to feel like something of a disaster. We come from a world of constant turmoil and activity. This is often all that most of us have ever known. While we may succeed in getting our bodies to stop, our minds often race on without us, jumping from one thing to the next like a toddler who's had too much sugar.

Turn your attention to the world around you. Sit by a stream and watch the water dance over the rocks, listen to the varied tones coming from different areas of the stream. Look closely at the grass and flowers, admire their form and breathe in their smell. Imagine what their days must be like. Then, notice the deep peace that emanates from all of nature, that surety and confidence of being that permeates the land.

If something urgent comes to mind, look at it for a moment until you know you've seen it, make a note to come back to it later, and then let it go. Let everything go except exactly what is before you. Let go of your need to accomplish anything right now, let go of your calendar and your schedule, let go of your own importance. Simply let yourself be for a while.

This is the way to begin your journey into silence and your innermost self. While it may seem like an unproductive waste of time, it is one of the most important things you can do. This stillness will slowly begin to re-tune and rewire you, enabling you to engage with what is truly important in life.

INWARD JOURNEY

One would think that as one grows older, our focus and our influence would naturally expand outward. This is the logical progression, yet the journey to a life of wholeness and integration requires what appears to be a major detour. It asks us to travel inward to our very core where we must walk the long, winding trails inside of us before they lead outward beyond the self. If this part of the journey is skipped, then all the outer activity tends to remain quite superficial, doing far less good than we might realize.

During early adulthood we are focused on doing things and being someone. We spend decades struggling to be recognized and accepted, to find our place. Yet when we finally arrive we find it to be but a mirage, an empty illusion. We have to go back and rethink our lives. The answers to who we are and how we should live are found in the hidden depths within. It might sound selfish and even foolish, but it is only by going deep within and finding these answers that we can truly go out into this world in a meaningful way.

Silence

Most of us think of space—that area between objects, between planets, stars, and everything—as nothingness, merely the absence of stuff. Scientists, however, are discovering that it is actually not empty at all but teeming with activity and filled with substances we don't yet fully understand. They currently think dark matter may be the primary component of our universe, when only a few years ago we didn't even know it existed. Dark matter is thought to be a real substance that has a significant impact on the world around us. One of the many things scientists are learning is that this dark matter may be pushing against the visible matter, moving our galaxies away from each other at an accelerating rate.

I've found that, in much the same way, most of us view silence as merely the absence of noise. We consider it to be empty and unnerving. Our first encounter with silence may be out in the woods, where all we can hear is the rustling of leaves or the singing of birds. This is a wonderful type of natural silence, but there are also deeper silences to be found, such as in the woods after a winter snow. Here your ears may not be able to detect any identifiable sound at all. It can be a little uncomfortable the first time, as all you may hear is the ringing in your ears, perhaps the sound of your own breath, and the movement of the fabrics you are wearing. If you take the time to just sit in such silence and listen, you may begin to realize that in the "emptiness" there is something there, something profound. There is a fullness, closeness, a presence behind all the outer acoustic and visual activity. Silence, like space, seems like emptiness or an absence. But it is actually the opposite. Everything else tends to mask the deeper substance of our world. Silence helps us see it and touch it.

*Mystery is not the absence of meaning, but the
presence of more meaning than we can comprehend.*

– DENNIS COVINGTON

Moonlight

One of the unavoidable aspects of my job as a landscape photographer is that after I finish photographing sunset at a backcountry lake, I then have to make my way through the darkness back to the trailhead where my vehicle is parked. During the summer months that journey is often many miles long, giving time for the sky to grow dark and the stars to appear. At times the moon rises and helps me find my way. Sometimes it can be so bright that I will turn off my headlamp and hike back to the trailhead without any artificial light. Most of the time, though, the moonlight is just bright enough to make out the rough outline of the trail, but everything else around it is in darkness. There could be a bear or a moose sitting right next to the trail and I wouldn't see it.

At times we live our lives by moonlight. Although we try to convince ourselves that we see clearly, there is so much about this world that remains a mystery. We often can't even express our own inner longings—the reason we took a particular action or why we responded so harshly to that comment by a co-worker. If we can't even understand our own hearts, how can we be so certain we understand others or the fullness of the world around us? Perhaps the healthiest position we can take is that of humility, a recognition that we view this world by moonlight.

In Perspective

Looking down from up on a mountain everything seems so miniature. It is almost as if none of it is actually real. The farther up I step the more insignificant it all seems. Roads and houses appear even smaller than letters on a page. Yet when I am down there it all seems so large. If I stand too close, my problems feel like towering peaks ready to crumble on top of me.

It appears that my perspective is not as objective as I would like to think. It is so influenced by where I stand and how I view things. In fact, even my varied perspectives are far from the only ways to see reality. Imagine the viewpoint of a microbe, an ant, a dog, a fish, a giraffe, an eagle, or even the Voyager spacecraft traveling at the edge of our solar system. They all perceive the world so very differently. None of them has a false perception, but they all are limited in their view of reality. Reality is far too complex for any one perspective to encompass it all. The cosmos stretches simultaneously in two opposite directions and perhaps many more. It appears to extend almost infinitely on the macro scale and so far we've not seen an end to the micro scale either.

So, what perspective should I hold? How should I view the reality of my situation? The only answer that makes sense to me is one of great humility. While there is much we do know, our perspective is biased and limited. While we continue to grow and learn, we must also embrace the mystery of never fully knowing.

MYSTERY

Much of the time I walk in the fog uncertain of where I am, unsure if I'm headed in the right direction or even moving at all. The dark clouds swirl in front of my face, leaving me nearly blind. But every once in a while, when I stop striving and simply sit in the stillness, a small window in the clouds opens for a moment, giving me a glimpse of where I am and where I need to head. It all becomes so clear. My heart fills with a deep sense of peace, and a weight I didn't even know was there falls away.

Oh, how I long to hold on to this moment, to always see things with clarity; however, the clouds soon move back in and I am tempted to doubt whether I actually saw anything at all. Yet somewhere deep down I know that I glimpsed my destination. In the darkness I begin to wonder why we are forced to live in such mystery. Could there be more to it than just some unavoidable frustration? Is it possible that mystery is somehow an essential component of our formation in our journey through life? If there is a chance this is true, then let us whole-heartedly embrace the often-uncomfortable mystery of life and let it work its good into us.

SCIENTIFIC VIEW

We live in a world where the scientific perspective dominates. As someone who loves the natural sciences, I find so much to celebrate. We've learned incredible things that have changed our lives and opened up vast new areas of understanding. We've conquered diseases, created devices that have transformed our world, and begun to understand the history of our universe. We've glimpsed worlds that are farther away than we can comprehend and we've even begun to understand the often-bizarre underpinnings of the cosmos. At times it seems as if there is nothing beyond the deductive power of the scientific method.

At the same time its passive, clinical approach seems to overlook or completely disregard many of the deeper aspects of human experience, the intangibles that make life worth living. Awe, wonder, beauty, and love are experiences that science may never fully understand. Science attempts to describe what things are and how they work. This, however, is only one way of knowing—an important yet superficial and distant way of knowing. It tends to disregard experience, emotion, and personal significance or it lumps these into artificial categories that rob them of their meaning.

As humans, we have the ability to be deeply moved by something as simple as snow-covered trees, the smile of a spouse, and the last glimmer of light at the end of the day. We all live with deep longings inside of us, longings for things that are not visible: for goodness, for wholeness, for transcendence, and for so much more. There is a rich inner world that seems to exceed the neurons in our head or our evolutionary development. Could there be a deeper something within all of us that is beyond our ability to dissect and study?

CLOUDY

There are many times when I am photographing up in the tundra that my attention is captured by the clouds. At one moment I may see what clearly looks like a dragon and then just a minute later it has vanished completely. Clouds are constantly changing. Though we can point and say, "There they are," we can't really define their edges—at least, not for long. They have a mysterious and almost ghostly quality to them. Perhaps that's why I find them so interesting.

When I look within myself, I find that my inner world is much the same. It seems to defy my attempts to draw its boundaries, to say this is where it starts and this is where it ends. It is a strange and nebulous world that seems to extend as deeply as the sky itself. It is filled with surprises, with beauty, and also with dark storms. There are some days when it seems completely inaccessible, as if the wind had blown it far away, leaving only blue emptiness. Then there are other days when it is so thick and substantive that it's hard to focus on the outer world.

This inner life we all have seems to be deeper and greater than our outer life yet we tend to give it little attention. We give our body food, drink, sleep and exercise, but what do we give to our inner life? Do we give it attention? Do we feed it with good things? Do we stretch it and explore it? Though it defies our boxes, there is an amazing beauty inside each of us that deserves our attention and thoughtful care.

Take it Slowly

Most days, I throw on my camera backpack and head up into the mountains. I typically have a destination in mind and am often racing against the clock to get there well before the sun rises. My mind and my legs are anxious to move quickly but within a few minutes I find myself breathless, struggling to get enough air into my lungs. At the high elevations of Colorado there is less air available and so even though my legs may be strong enough to keep going at a rapid pace, my lungs can't keep up. I know that if I slow down to a point where I can easily breathe I will be able to keep moving all day without tiring. Yet something inside still tries to move faster than my lungs can support. It is a game I will never win. I need to learn to let my lungs set the pace.

In much the same way, I tend to stuff my head with information without waiting for my heart. Knowledge that is undigested and unapplied is mostly meaningless. Until we learn to live what we know, it remains trivia. Our hearts and minds must learn to travel together. It seems as if all the truly important things of life happen so much more slowly than we would like. We live fast-paced lives with slow-speed souls. Bringing the two into sync is the hard-won secret of those who have allowed life to mature them.

THE RIVER

As I made my way down from a high mountain pass, I came across a small stream at its source. The water was bouncing from rock to rock in a joyful manner as it made its way downward. For the next ten miles this stream and I traveled together. It was ever changing as it encountered the varied terrain along the way. As I walked beside it my mind began to wander and wonder what this stream might be thinking if it were mortal.

When this stream slowed down, drifting back and forth without any sense of progress or purpose through a gentle meadow, would it wonder if its best days were behind it? Would it remember those early cascades with their exciting roar and think that its ride was mostly over?

I knew what this young river could not. I knew its future, but I had no way to tell it that it was only at the very start of an epic journey. Ahead lay deep forests, raging cascades, deep dark canyons, and quiet meadows. Beyond that it would join with other rivers and cross the Great Plains, growing in size until it was the mightiest river in the nation, eventually becoming the Gulf of Mexico and then the Atlantic Ocean.

Life is often like this. We are unable to see over the horizon of the moment. It can be tempting to extrapolate the present and assume that life will continue just as it is, but rarely is it ever that straightforward. Get out of the eddy and into the flow. Let it take you on an unexpected journey into becoming who you were meant to be.

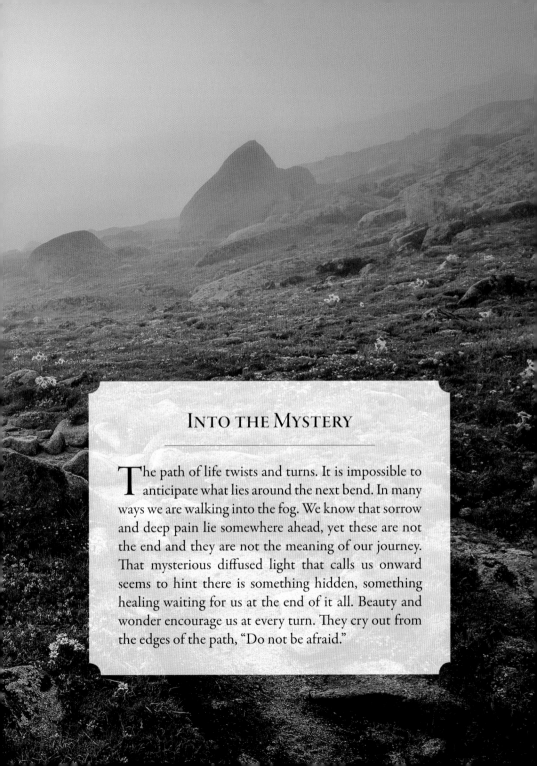

INTO THE MYSTERY

The path of life twists and turns. It is impossible to anticipate what lies around the next bend. In many ways we are walking into the fog. We know that sorrow and deep pain lie somewhere ahead, yet these are not the end and they are not the meaning of our journey. That mysterious diffused light that calls us onward seems to hint there is something hidden, something healing waiting for us at the end of it all. Beauty and wonder encourage us at every turn. They cry out from the edges of the path, "Do not be afraid."

WATERFALL

I love waterfalls. I love their sound. I love the fresh cool air that comes off of them. I love the beautiful ribbon of white that contrasts with the rock around them. I love everything about them and often spend time sitting in their presence contemplating life. On a recent encounter with one, I began to realize that a waterfall is unlike a tree, a mountain, or a lake. It is something ephemeral. It exists only in the moment as drops of water divide from the stream and tumble through the air. They appear for just a second or two and then they are gone. You can let them run through your fingers, but unlike sand you can never pick up the same drop again. It is gone, vanished back into the larger stream from which it came.

Life is a lot like standing under a waterfall. Each moment comes at us so quickly and then before we even realize it, it is gone, never to be experienced again. When we are young we try desperately to hold on to these moments, but it is always futile. We can't stop, hold, or control any of these drops that fall into our lives. Perhaps part of maturity is learning to open our hands in welcome, choosing to relish the way each moment of life washes over us, at peace with the knowledge that what life brings is outside of our control. The only control we have is how we choose to respond to it. Much like a waterfall, when we step back and look at the whole of it, we realize this fleeting life is exquisitely beautiful.

*Darkness is the great canvas against
which beauty becomes visible.*

– JOHN O'DONOHUE

Through the Darkness

As we begin the path toward wholeness it usually leads us first into the darkness, where we come face-to-face with those things we would most like to avoid. Many who begin the journey encounter this and quickly turn back. Yet the path to wholeness has no alternate route. We must first walk through our own darkness before we can come out on the other side where the shining sun and peace patiently wait to welcome us.

The Dark Night

At the end of the day after the sun has set and the color fades from the sky, darkness, which has been waiting just beyond the horizon, seizes its opportunity and descends like a heavy blanket. The gorgeous mountains around me disappear from my sight despite my longing to hold them in view. With their joyful and vibrant colors, the flowers at my feet darken and then vanish. As I make my way along the trail, thick clouds blow in, blocking any light from the world above. I am cut off, alone. It isn't long before fatigue and exhaustion set in. The growing cold and seemingly endless sharp rocks prevent any opportunity for rest.

Alone in the blackness, my thoughts do not ascend to the heights but seem to spiral downward toward a thick sadness. The cares of the world crawl out from their hiding places and descend upon me without mercy. Every pain of my life, every failure, every unmet longing confronts me in the dark with no sign of relief. I'm losing all sense of time and place. Where did light go? Where did goodness go?

I long to throw off the heaviness and return to the sunshine, but I find myself powerless to do so. What can I do? How do I end the darkness? It is not mine to end, for I do not control the sun. So I will wait patiently in the pain. I will not fight it, but neither will I give myself over to it. No, I will look to the east and wait for that first hint of light on the horizon. I don't know if my wait will be long or short, but I will patiently wait. I will wait in hope, for darkness has no choice but to give way to the coming sun.

DESOLATION

At times the sun is obscured, hidden from our sight, and thick clouds swirl around us. Hope fades and it seems that all is dark. It's in these times of desolation I remember the words scrawled on a cellar by a Jew in hiding during World War II: "I believe in the sun, even when it isn't shining. I believe in love, even when I do not feel it. I believe in God, even when he is silent."

FALLEN LEAVES

Just yesterday the sun was shining. Golden aspen leaves glittered under the deep blue sky while birds sang, elk bugled, and the glassy lakes reflected it all as if to say, "Look at all this!" It was as if the whole world had finally been set right. Then, around midday, clouds could be seen building just behind the mountains. Each hour they grew in size and darkness until their blackness hid the sun. Soon a violent and bitterly cold wind rushed down the slopes, through the valleys and into town. It snatched the golden leaves and hurled them to the ground. Animals took shelter and visitors left the park as the trees groaned under the strain of the howling wind. This was the beginning of winter's offensive, robbing the world of color and joy. It will be a long time until any color returns, certainly not for at least six months, perhaps seven.

We are like those leaves that are held on by a tiny brittle stem. How fragile and precious our little lives are. Just when all seems to finally be going well, we are caught off guard by tragedy. We find that our security was an illusion. No matter how hard we cling to life, we are not as powerful as we want to believe. Perhaps some of us will hold on longer than those next to us, but in the end we will all fall. The winter is inevitable.

Yet the trees know something we do not. They know about winter—the loss, the pain, the loneliness—but they also know about spring. They put their hope not in endless winter, but in the coming resurrection of May and June.

LIMBLESS

The death of a family member or friend is like having a limb brutally ripped from one's body. It leaves a gaping wound and a deep sense of loss. It is an injury that does not easily heal. Years from now the large scars will not have faded and if you touch them just right they will still send a sharp pang of pain into your deepest being.

When I walk through an aspen forest and see their many scars from limbs that once were, I feel as if I am in the company of those who understand. I too carry these deep black marks and they will follow me through life as reminders of what once was. Each mark holds so many memories—some sweet, some hilarious, some hard, and some that seem to be fading from my sight with each passing year.

As I look through the forest from one tree to the next I see that there is not one here who doesn't carry those scars. Even the young ones show signs of some type of loss. As humans we can more easily disguise our wounds. Though they aren't visible on the surface we can be fairly certain that most people we meet carry some of that same aching pain we do.

Grief is a certainty in this life, so we must live with compassion not only for others but also for ourselves. We must be gracious and tender toward all who carry the pains of this world.

CHINOOK

This past December and January were glorious winter months with unusual amounts of snow. As a skier and lover of winter, I was thrilled to be able to ski up to the top of a mountain after work and enjoy floating down on a pillow of powder. My son celebrated the winter weather by creating a big snow hill at the top of our driveway with a bobsled-like track for his plastic sled. It looked like we would have the best winter yet.

One night I awoke to hear the winds blow with such fierceness that the trees began to bend and break. Many giant ponderosa trees, more than a hundred years old, fell under the strength of the gale. These winds were not only fierce but very warm. Within hours the snowpack began to recede and within a few days nearly all the snow in the lower valleys was gone and much was lost in the mountains as well. The Chinook winds swept in and carried it away, leaving an ugly brown world in its wake.

Who of us hasn't experienced the same thing with our plans and dreams? What had seemed so certain one day was gone overnight, taking our hopes along with it. The sense of loss and disorientation is often profound. In the blink of an eye we find ourselves in a situation we never anticipated. So, what now? How do we move forward with our carefully crafted plans in ruins? Perhaps we need to open our hands and let go, for only then can we receive the unexpected goodness when it appears in that empty space.

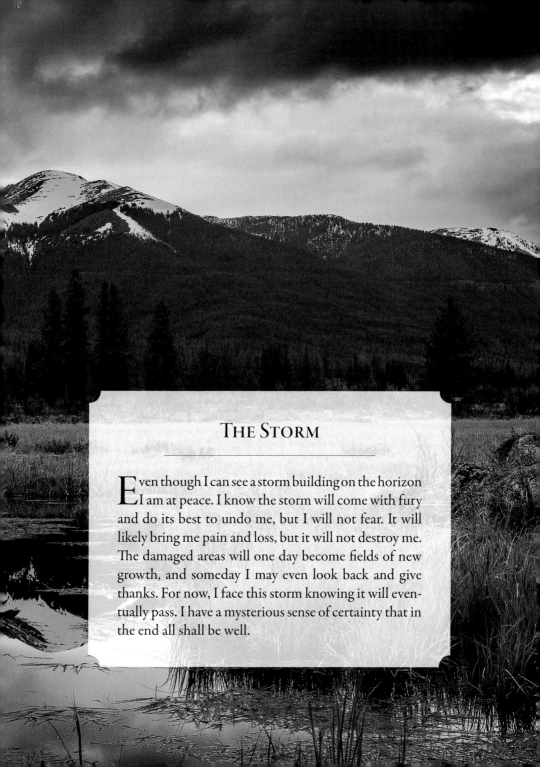

THE STORM

Even though I can see a storm building on the horizon I am at peace. I know the storm will come with fury and do its best to undo me, but I will not fear. It will likely bring me pain and loss, but it will not destroy me. The damaged areas will one day become fields of new growth, and someday I may even look back and give thanks. For now, I face this storm knowing it will eventually pass. I have a mysterious sense of certainty that in the end all shall be well.

The wound is the place where the Light enters you.

– RUMI

The Gift

When I was eight years old I had a plan to save the world's wild creatures from the ravages of humanity by designing a rocket ship to take them to another planet. When I was fourteen I decided to live to help people most in need in our world. All through my teens and twenties I strove to make the biggest splash I could with this life of mine, to leave the world better than I found it. In my early thirties my grand dreams were confronted by reality. The reality was not the difficulties presented by the world, but those I encountered in myself. I was not as strong as I thought. I regularly suffered from health issues as a result of stress; I was unable to cope with all that was constantly required of me and long days without rest. Eventually I experienced an internal breakdown.

When I finally collapsed in 2003, I felt as if I had failed. The following years were dark and heavy. In that deep silence, in the emptiness and pain, I had to wrestle with hard questions that challenged the core of who I thought I was and how I was supposed to live. When I finally engaged with those questions, they sent me down a rabbit hole into a whole new world that turned me upside down and inside out. The superficial was washed away and my roots began to go down deep. Those dark years became the greatest gift I've ever been given.

If you are facing something similar, don't ignore the hard questions being asked of you in the pain and darkness. They may be a hidden gift.

FIRE

In 2012 an illegal campfire in Rocky Mountain National Park started a major wildfire. Three thousand acres were burned and on one night it raced up through Moraine Park, worrying residents along the eastern edge of Estes Park. When the fire was finally put out at a cost of six million dollars, all that was left was thick gray ash. During the next years when I would hike through the area, each footstep would send clouds of ash into the air. All that could be seen were dead tree trunks and devastating ash. It was a dreadful situation.

On my most recent visit I was delighted to see that almost all of the ashy ground was covered in wildflowers, as well as a large variety of plants and many new trees. What was once ugly devastation was now thriving and would become an even more beautiful forest than before.

As I spent time there I realized how much this area reminded me of the tragedies in our lives. Terrible things happen that leave us devastated and without hope. All we once had is lost and can never be regained. For years we may live hollow lives filled with mourning. Then slowly, somewhere along the way, when we least expect it, life begins expressing itself anew in ways we would never have guessed. It is in no way a return to what was, but in its place the arrival of something different. It is the beginning of a new chapter—a beautiful chapter in our lives we thought would never be possible. As we look back, it's not that we are glad for the tragedy, but we realize this new place of beauty would not have been possible without it.

ENTER THE PAIN

Long quiet trails can be places of incredible peace, but just as often they can be places of intense pain. Most of us have hidden wounds we don't really think about during our daily lives. Our constant activity keeps them from reaching the surface. Perhaps that is one of the reasons we remain so busy, to avoid these places of pain inside.

A long quiet trail can unmask these wounds like nothing else. Much like a blister in the boot, these sources of internal pain rise to the surface until they begin to scream in our ears and ignoring them is no longer an option.

While our tendency is to avoid the intense discomfort, this pain is actually a call to healing. Our broken relationships, our fears, our hidden wounds need not fester. The pain calls us to pay attention, to lean in to our wounds and address them head on so healing can flow into these areas. When we discover this, the discomfort revealed by the trail becomes our friend and we realize that the real path we are on is the path to wholeness.

MOMENTARILY MALLEABLE

On the western end of Rocky Mountain National Park is a portion of the Never Summer Mountains that was formed through volcanic activity. It is thought Mount Richthofen is actually the remnant of an ancient volcano. It's easy to picture that when you see it today.

As I thought about these seemingly unchanging mountains I realized there was a period in their history where instead of being solid and stable they were actually fluid and changeable. There was no certainty as to what their current shape would be. The intense heat deep below the surface of the earth melted the rock, which could then become almost any shape imaginable.

For most of our time on this planet, we can do little to change who we are. Try as we might we tend to stay the same. However, in those times of intense crisis, those times we all wish would never come, that hardness deep within us softens. Although we may not realize it, in the midst of a crisis we become momentarily malleable. Our responses in the heat shape us more than any other time in our lives. If we give in to anger and bitterness, they will define much of our life from this point forward. Alternatively, if in the pain we turn toward acceptance, forgiveness, gratitude, or humility these often become defining characteristics of the next phase of our life. Perhaps these excruciating crises give us a momentary opportunity to choose our own unique shape.

Nothing Wasted

As I look back over the course of my life there are so many things I would rather forget—the loss of my father at an early age, the taunts of other kids who misunderstood me, the pain I almost allowed to swallow me, and the terrible unkindness I showed at times to my brother and sister, who were going through their own journeys of pain. Even in my older years I look back on many things with sadness. There are years I feel I have wasted. I am pretty sure I'm not alone in these feelings that painfully pierce my inner being.

As I walk through the forests to find their comfort I notice a different way of looking at things. The late-autumn ground is not bare; it is covered in fallen leaves and branches. There is also scat left by deer and rabbits, dead grass, and even the carcass of a squirrel that recently died. All around me are signs of pain, loss, and ugliness. Yet for the forest this is not the end of the story. For here nothing is ever wasted. It is all absorbed into the forest floor, providing nourishment for life. Without all of this loss, the forest couldn't grow.

Could it be the same for us that nothing is truly wasted? Could it be possible that our pain and failures lay the foundation for our growth? I wonder who I might have become without having gone through the suffering and without having faced my own failures. I am fairly certain that without these I would not be where I am today. Perhaps I need to look more kindly on these areas I've always tried to ignore.

True to the Core

Life is a journey of becoming. It is not about appeasing our appetites until we die; rather, it is a long road of becoming true. Much of our younger lives are spent trying to fit in and become like everyone else. In that process we lose not only our own unique preferences and sense of self but also something of the essence of who we are. As we grow older we find that the form we've taken on isn't our own. It helps us fit in and move through society, but there is this sense of it not really belonging to us.

If we are to grow toward health we have to begin to break free from all that isn't real in our lives. This involves an uncomfortable honesty and vulnerability. It requires us to look deep within to identify our deepest longings and desires. Perhaps we will find we have a desire to write or paint or travel or compose music or write a book. This is a great start, but it is not our deepest self. We need to search until we can see the deeper, more foundational desire behind these surface desires. This is the place from which we need to live.

When we live from a place of integrity with our deepest selves, we will find that all the outer aspects begin to fall into place. Being true both inside and out means we have to face many things within that we wish were not there. But it is in facing them that we grow. This is the journey of transformation and healing—the true journey of life.

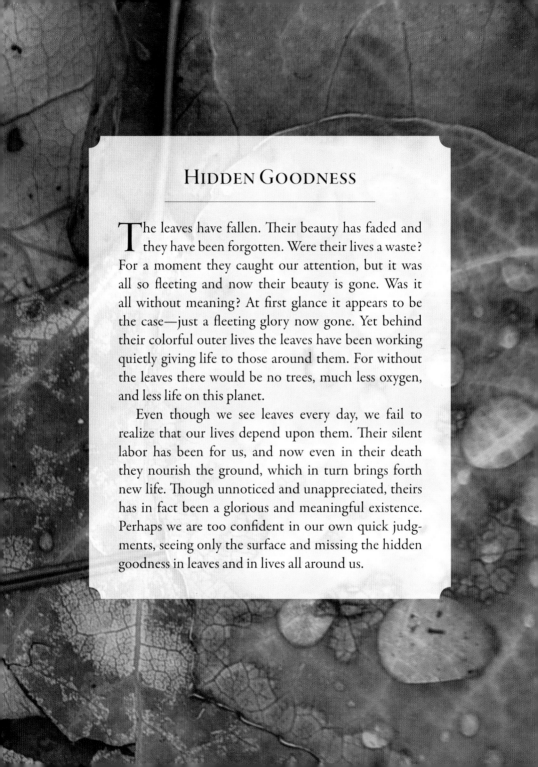

HIDDEN GOODNESS

The leaves have fallen. Their beauty has faded and they have been forgotten. Were their lives a waste? For a moment they caught our attention, but it was all so fleeting and now their beauty is gone. Was it all without meaning? At first glance it appears to be the case—just a fleeting glory now gone. Yet behind their colorful outer lives the leaves have been working quietly giving life to those around them. For without the leaves there would be no trees, much less oxygen, and less life on this planet.

Even though we see leaves every day, we fail to realize that our lives depend upon them. Their silent labor has been for us, and now even in their death they nourish the ground, which in turn brings forth new life. Though unnoticed and unappreciated, theirs has in fact been a glorious and meaningful existence. Perhaps we are too confident in our own quick judgments, seeing only the surface and missing the hidden goodness in leaves and in lives all around us.

Assumptions

Mountains are things of wonder. They stand so tall, shooting up out of the plains and into the clouds. You can't help but gasp the first time you see one. For many who live along Colorado's Front Range, they have the privilege of waking each morning to a view of Longs Peak, one of the tallest mountains in Colorado. If you asked those fortunate folks if they could identify Longs Peak in a photo, they would think it was a silly question, for they know this mountain and feel they would instantly recognize it.

But mountains are not as obvious and predictable as we might think. Our perception of them depends more on our own perspective than we might realize. Simply travel to the south side of Longs Peak and it now looks like a completely different mountain that few people would recognize; the same is true of the view from the west and the north. I've found that mountains also look completely different when we are far away and when we are viewing them up close. These changes of perspective can make low-lying ridges look like tall summits and can completely confuse the relationship of one mountain to another.

If we struggle so much to perceive the truth of an unmoving granite mountain, how much more could we be mistaken about those with whom we come into contact each day—moving, breathing people with deep and complex inner lives. It is so easy to assume that our perspective gives us an accurate picture of them. We make judgments and decisions about how to treat them based on what we think we see. Perhaps the mighty mountains should cause us to stop in our tracks and feel a deep sense of humility, for they are clear reminders of how limited our perceptions are. Perhaps we would be better off not to allow ourselves to jump to judgment and instead allow ourselves to be surprised by the beautiful complexity and mystery of each other.

Contentment

Have you ever hiked into a grove of aspen trees in order to just sit with them and hide from the world under their canopy? There is almost nothing better to do, especially on a warm autumn day. Here you can watch the sunlight find its way through the leaves and be transformed into the most warm and delicious light. If you stay still you will soon hear the rustling of the leaves in the wind and understand why they are often referred to as trembling aspen, as the slightest breath of wind will cause the leaves to shake.

As I sit and watch these trees I realize that an aspen never seeks to be the best, the most productive, the most famous, the tallest or most slender. Rather, an aspen is content with itself, with gathering sunlight from the sky, soaking up moisture from the ground, and living in harmony with its widespread family of aspen. As a result it lives a life of peace, contentment, and profound beauty.

How very different it is for us human beings. We have a tendency to try to stand out, to be someone. If I were to guess, I would say that most of this comes from a sense of insecurity. Somewhere within we feel we don't belong or that we aren't good enough. We go to great lengths to prove to ourselves that we are special. What if we changed our perspective and viewed ourselves as already belonging just as we are. Perhaps we might then find the same sense of well-being and beauty as the aspen.

EYES WIDE OPEN

My days are probably similar to yours. The alarm clock goes off and my mind quickly fills with thoughts of all that is on my plate. There are numerous deadlines to be met, places I need to be, people I need to speak to, and correspondence that is piling up like mountain snow. Some days I simply want to go back to bed and forget it all. At times I get stressed and even depressed by the never-ending string of demands.

When I am finally able to pull away for an hour and walk in the quietness of the woods my stress begins to fall to the side of the trail, my muscles relax, and thankfully I regain some perspective on my life. Slowly I recognize that the areas of frustration and difficulty had captured my full attention. My vision had so narrowed that I was blinded to everything else that surrounded me. I missed the laughter of my son, the smell of the ponderosa, the beauty of the falling snow, the kindness of a stranger, and a thousand other moments of goodness in my day. All I could see were the problems.

My life, probably like yours, is filled with unacknowledged goodness. In order to live a life of wholeness, I need to pay attention to the wider reality. This is not some sort of happiness gimmick or positive-thinking technique; it is recognizing that my life consists of more goodness and joy than I am usually aware of. While the pain, frustrations, and deadlines still exist, they are only a part of a much bigger whole. If I pay attention, I have many reasons to get out of bed this morning.

STRETCH

Here in America we tend to be focused on speed and efficiency. We aim for the moon and then race to get there before anyone else. We speak into our phones and instantly have an answer for almost any question. We order food and are served within minutes. Every day our technology increases and enables us to do more and more at an ever-faster rate. As a result, our lives move at light speed. It's not surprising that we so easily become frustrated with our internal lives. They don't change on a dime and there is no technology that will quickly accomplish the growth we long for. No, our deepest selves cannot be controlled in this way. They are more like mighty trees that grow slowly, dependent upon the nutrients and light they are given.

Every day the spruce tree reaches upward toward the sun, welcoming each ray of light. Though it may feel as if it is making no progress and will never reach its goal, each day of stretching in the same direction is not in vain. Without knowing it, and without any daily sign of progress, it grows from tiny seedling to towering wonder.

Be patient with yourself; take time to feed your soul with good things. Never stop reaching toward the light. Trust in the slow work of growth and pay no attention to progress, for true progress will happen without you ever realizing it.

Men go abroad to wonder at the heights of mountains, at the huge waves of the sea, at the long courses of the rivers, at the vast compass of the ocean, at the circular motions of the stars, and they pass by themselves without wondering. .

– AUGUSTINE OF HIPPO

HARD WON BEAUTY

As I've hiked and explored the wilderness over the years, I often stumble across scenes of extraordinary beauty. Sometimes the scene consists of a fascinating rock that has been sculpted by the wind or a flower growing on a small island in the middle of a rushing stream. Sometimes it's a waterfall created by an ancient break in the earth or a shoreline that has been carved by the pounding sea.

What I've begun to realize is that the places of greatest beauty are not typically those where life has been smooth and stable; rather, beauty seems to spring from difficult and tumultuous situations. Bob Dylan knew what he was saying when he wrote, "Behind every beautiful thing there's been some kind of pain."

While I sit and admire an old twisted pine that has grown on a rocky cliff face, I see how it has to struggle to survive. It has had to reach down through small cracks in the rock, putting its roots much farther down into the depths than other trees. At the same time, it has been exposed to the high winds and storms while also relying on fewer nutrients. Somehow, because of all this, it grew to become a thing of beauty. As I look on in awe I'm filled with hope that the difficulties of life don't have to destroy us but can lead to a unique and unexpected beauty within.

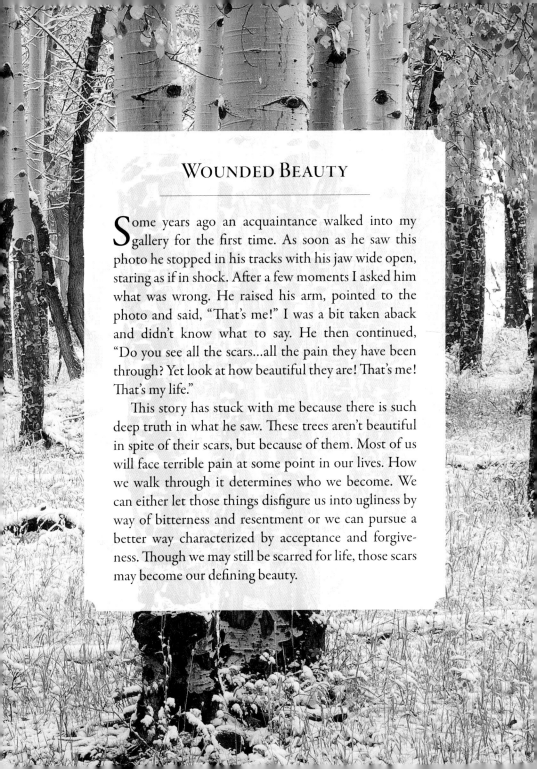

WOUNDED BEAUTY

Some years ago an acquaintance walked into my gallery for the first time. As soon as he saw this photo he stopped in his tracks with his jaw wide open, staring as if in shock. After a few moments I asked him what was wrong. He raised his arm, pointed to the photo and said, "That's me!" I was a bit taken aback and didn't know what to say. He then continued, "Do you see all the scars...all the pain they have been through? Yet look at how beautiful they are! That's me! That's my life."

This story has stuck with me because there is such deep truth in what he saw. These trees aren't beautiful in spite of their scars, but because of them. Most of us will face terrible pain at some point in our lives. How we walk through it determines who we become. We can either let those things disfigure us into ugliness by way of bitterness and resentment or we can pursue a better way characterized by acceptance and forgiveness. Though we may still be scarred for life, those scars may become our defining beauty.

BECOME BEAUTIFUL

As a photographer I spend quite a bit of time searching for beauty, trying to find those scenes that speak to something deep inside me. As I've done this, I have come to the point where I am not satisfied with simply photographing beauty, but I recognize within myself an intense longing to actually become beautiful. I think it is a hidden desire shared by all of humanity. I am not speaking about some superficial appearance of beauty, but something much deeper. Irish philosopher and poet John O'Donohue says, "Beauty isn't all just about niceness, loveliness. Beauty is about more rounded substantial becoming." So what does this mean? How does one become beautiful? Here are a few brief ideas based on my pursuit of beauty through photography:

Live in vibrant contrast to your environment. Forget about fitting in. Instead, unashamedly pursue what you know to be good in your own unique way. Don't seek to be seen or praised. Simply ignore the onlookers.

Be real and avoid all forms of falseness. Focus on becoming your own true self. Listen and pursue that deep internal calling. It won't lead you astray.

Live with openness and expectation despite the storms of life. Do not let yourself grow hard or bitter. Do not build walls around yourself. Embrace the pain and see it through. Dare to live vulnerably in this harsh world.

WINTER'S REST

For many, there is a deep sadness associated with the arrival of winter. In many ways this is understandable: the color is gone from the earth and the trees, leaving the world looking brown and gray. Soon the cold winter winds arrive with a bite, followed by snow that has to be shoveled from the driveway before leaving for work. Yet for the natural world, winter is not a time of sadness, but a time of rest. Many creatures such as bears, bees, marmots, and mice hibernate during the winter months. Other creatures like the elk and deer do not hibernate but take a slower, more restful approach to life. Even trees go dormant over the winter, no longer creating food and no longer growing but simply resting until the arrival of spring.

When our world was more agriculturally based, we also took part in this slowing down during the dark winter months. Today the wonders of technology have deprived us of this winter rest. Now we are just as busy in January as we were in July. There is no longer a place for rest in our lives. While we might be more "productive" without slower periods in life, we may find that we lack depth and creativity. Too much pushing without slowing down leaves us hollow and shallow. Perhaps there is something we can learn from the natural world. Perhaps our modern world has missed something important in its push toward production and progress. Perhaps we all need more winter in our lives.

FUTURE SIGHT

No matter who we are or where we are born, we grow up with unrecognized preconceptions about life. Our culture has a massive influence on how we understand ourselves, each other, and the world around us. However, its influence is completely invisible until we find a way to step outside our own cultural boxes. If we do this, we may be shocked by the confines of our cultural perceptions. We don't see nearly as fully as we thought; no culture does, for each has its own unique blinders.

One of the key traits of our Western culture is that we tend to be future-oriented. We live our lives planning, dreaming, and reaching for tomorrow. While there are many benefits to this, one of the things we lose in the process is today. We have trouble savoring the moment we're in. We find it difficult to slow down and experience where we are right now.

The natural world can help pull us into the present. Its very nature causes us to slow down as it gently calls us to listen to the birds singing, to bend down and smell the flowers by the path, and to watch the sunlight break through the forest canopy. The forest encourages us to let go of tomorrow and embrace what is happening right this moment, letting the future and all other things that distract us from now fade back into the fog.

MOUNTAINS

Though they are the very definition of unmovable, mountains have the ability to move my soul in a way that almost nothing else can. They cause something deep within me to well up with emotion and want to sing. They reveal my smallness yet inspire me to be more. Though they speak not a single word, they say so much to the core of my being. Somehow my soul seems to be rooted in the mountains. They are part of my being and I in some way feel part of them as well.

THE TRAIL

I absolutely love to look at trail photos. They pull me into the photo and at the same time into myself. As I look at the image, I begin to wonder what lies over the horizon. There is a sense of excitement about the possibilities that could unfold with each step forward. I have that same sense of excitement when I'm on a new trail, but experience has taught me the bends in the trail sometimes take me into difficult and dangerous terrain rather than the peaceful meadow I had imagined.

Many of the trails I hike in Rocky Mountain National Park begin in gentle meadows, sometimes following gurgling streams, but as I keep going the terrain is constantly changing. Before I know it, the trail may be hugging the side of a mountain with steep drops, or it may lead me up into the tundra high above the trees where there is no protection from the howling winds and summer storms before dropping down into the calm forest again. If you follow a trail far enough you will experience the best and worst it has to offer.

When the trail is rough, I try to remind myself it won't stay that way. I just need to keep moving forward. Likewise when I'm in a peaceful meadow I begin to mentally prepare myself for the challenges that must surely lie ahead. It is so tempting to think that the way life is today is the way it will be in the future; the reality is that the trail of life is anything but consistent. Living with an awareness of the coming change keeps us from being caught off guard and enables us to live a more consistent life of peace.

INCALCULABLY RARE

During the mid-1800s, following the California Gold Rush, prospectors turned their sights on Colorado, including the area that is now Rocky Mountain National Park. They searched for telltale signs of gold in the rocks and dug numerous mines from Longs Peak to the Never Summer Mountains in hopes of finding the vein of gold that would make them rich.

What is it that makes gold so valuable? It is its rarity. In a 2011 letter to investors, Warren Buffett, one of the world's wealthiest people, estimated the total amount of gold that has been unearthed in all of human history could fit into one 67-foot cube!

As I gaze up at the stars with a sense of wonder I'm reminded we have hundreds of scientists searching that vastness for life—life of any kind, even microbial life. So far, we have not yet found any living thing. It may be out there, but if it is, it is likely very, very far from us. Our blue planet is teeming with life. Like a single nugget of gold in a vast desert, we are rich beyond measure and don't know it.

Not only are you and I things of rare wonder, so are the trees that grow in every shape and description, so is the world of insects, the grasses, fish, and even lichen on the rocks. If we pay attention, life is everywhere on this planet and none of it should be taken for granted. All life is a gift worthy of celebration.

Constant Companion

I've spent more than a decade as a student of light. Just as a baker primarily works with flour, photographers primarily work with light. For a photographer, light is even more important than the actual subject of a photograph. Light is what makes the object visible and at the same time creates the emotion of an image.

As I began to study light I realized most of us live our lives completely oblivious to the light that surrounds us every day. We fail to notice its varied colors and many moods. It is our constant but unrecognized companion. Even on the darkest of nights it is still there if we stop and let our eyes adjust. Though the light may appear very dim at times, it never leaves us.

In my life, light has become a symbol of hope. It reminds me that there is nowhere I can go where goodness and beauty cannot be found. Even in the bleakest of situations darkness never fully overcomes the light. This gives me hope not only for myself in the midst of the challenges I face but also for all who run from the light. Even the cruelest and most evil-seeming person cannot hide from its rays. Goodness and mercy will pursue them as long as they breathe. There is always hope both for others and for ourselves.

Eyesight of Friends

One of the funniest experiences I've had in Rocky Mountain National Park occurred just after Christmas of 2012. I was hiking up toward Mill Creek Basin on a cold, snowy morning. As I crested a hill, up ahead I saw two people sitting down and talking together. They were dressed in full arctic gear as if they were on an expedition to the North Pole. As I approached I greeted them and we fell into a conversation. I learned that this was their first time ever in the snow. They seemed extremely uncomfortable being out in the wilderness and told me they were a little lost. As we were talking, my eyes drifted down to the ground next to them where something had caught my sight. It was the antler of a bull elk. Then it dawned on me that the antler was still attached to the body of the elk it belonged to. It had obviously just recently died and was partially covered in snow. The people I was talking to were sitting on the body, having mistaken it for a log! When I pointed this out to them their first reaction was disbelief. But when they realized it was true they jumped up in terror, taking off down the trail and out of sight.

I'm often just like these folks, ignorant of where I actually am and what is happening around me. Close friends can sometimes see my situation more clearly than I can. They are able to point out things I have missed and can help me navigate areas that are unfamiliar to me. I in turn do the same for them. We need each other, more often than our individualistic natures like to admit.

RESTLESS

My heart is restless, longing after something different than I have. I want change, that new thing, comfort, entertainment, variety in my life. I am not happy here, but I'm sure I will be over there.

What madness fills my mind and propels me onward ever seeking, ever accumulating? We all know deep down when we buy that thing, when we reach that goal, when we've had that experience we will then be right back where we are today, looking over the fence at what we don't have. It is our human version of the gerbil wheel; despite all the energy expended, it leads nowhere.

Contentment, if it is to be found, can be found right here in our present circumstances. Peace does not dangle from an unreachable string; it is found when we give up the chase and recognize that we are surrounded by unnoticed blessings on every side. As we begin to realize the goodness of where we already are, restlessness fades and peace begins to grow.

The soul does not grow by addition but by subtraction.

– MEISTER ECKHART

WEIGHTLESS

On a winter's day there is almost nothing I would rather do than grab my skis and head up into the mountains. Being alone in the white stillness is a restorative experience. Even though it is hard work to pull my body up to the top of the mountain in the snow, it allows me to go within and reflect. When I finally get to the top, high above the forest, I turn my skis downward and begin to float over the snow as it silently gives way beneath my skis. There is an incredible sense of weightless freedom that simply cannot be described in words.

Sometimes, however, my goal is to photograph a sunset on top of a mountain. This means I must carry an extra thirty-five pounds of photo gear on my back. I can feel it from the moment I depart and it seems to get heavier with each mile, making the journey to the top slow and tiring. You would think that on my ski back down I could enjoy it, but the weight pulls me from side to side, causing me to lose my balance. I often end up upside down on my back, unable to get up until I finally release the straps and drop the pack.

There have been many times in my life where I've carried similar loads that have weighed me down and made life miserable. At times I try to carry things such as anger and resentment, which do nothing but destroy me from within. When I look closely at what I'm carrying inside, I begin to see that most of these burdens are needless weight. It is time for me to let them go and experience the weightless freedom that is right here waiting for me to embrace it.

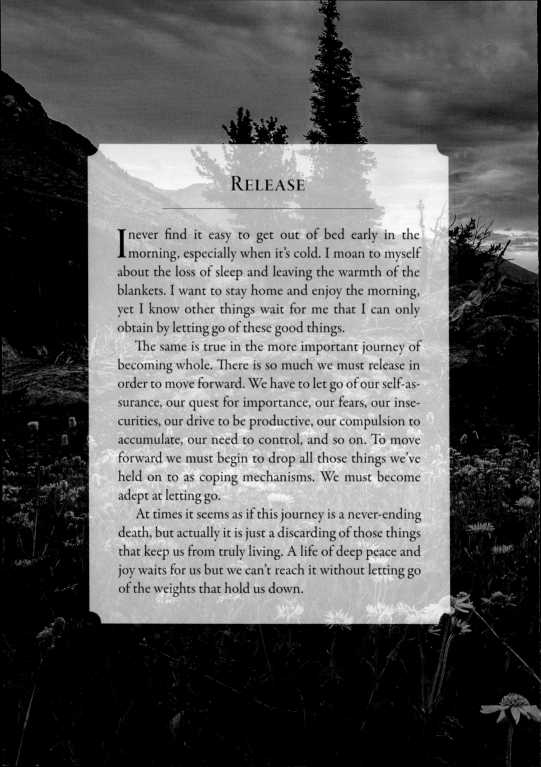

RELEASE

I never find it easy to get out of bed early in the morning, especially when it's cold. I moan to myself about the loss of sleep and leaving the warmth of the blankets. I want to stay home and enjoy the morning, yet I know other things wait for me that I can only obtain by letting go of these good things.

The same is true in the more important journey of becoming whole. There is so much we must release in order to move forward. We have to let go of our self-assurance, our quest for importance, our fears, our insecurities, our drive to be productive, our compulsion to accumulate, our need to control, and so on. To move forward we must begin to drop all those things we've held on to as coping mechanisms. We must become adept at letting go.

At times it seems as if this journey is a never-ending death, but actually it is just a discarding of those things that keep us from truly living. A life of deep peace and joy waits for us but we can't reach it without letting go of the weights that hold us down.

THE GRIP

In the autumn the aspen trees are breathtaking. They stand dressed in the finest coat of color one could imagine. You can't help but look at them with a sense of awe. Yet when the autumn winds arrive, the branches are quickly stripped bare. Every little twig stands naked and fully exposed. Their beauty is gone and no one pays them any attention. As much as they might have wanted to, they were unable to hold on to their leaves.

As I look back on my life, I am reminded of the dreams for the future I once held. I had it all planned out. From the outside they were beautiful and impressive, but the unexpected circumstances of life swept them away, leaving me empty, lost, and confused. I experienced years of great pain as I mourned what was lost, yet for the first time I was able to see clearly. Wrong motivations and twisted ideas of importance lay exposed at my feet. I had focused on the temporary externals and neglected what was most important.

I realized my fierce grip on the future was killing me and so I began to open my hands. Soon life began to flow again. The beauty returned but in a very different way than before, for it sprang from within. I realized the winter winds would come again, but now I was ready to be laid bare, for I finally understood that my life was in the trunk and not in the leaves.

PINECONES

During the winter months the pinecones on the ponderosa trees begin to open, releasing the seeds they have so closely guarded until now. This opening coincides with the winter winds, which often howl for months on end. The trees now have no control of their offspring. They entrust their seeds to the invisible wind to plant them where they may. They release all control and yet generation after generation they flourish. We, however, grasp and cling to our lives, possessions, and loved ones, trusting only that which we can see and control. Yet if you listen, you will hear the wind in the trees calling out to us too, encouraging us to release our seemingly desperate need for control.

INVISIBLE CHAINS

This morning I hiked toward a high mountain lake. About two-thirds of the way there I realized I had forgotten my extra water, sunscreen, sunglasses, and other important things in my truck. It was going to be a very hot day, so I did the wise thing and headed back down without reaching my destination. As I walked down the trail I felt uneasy inside. I tried to clarify my feelings and find their source; I realized that I felt embarrassed and ashamed for not reaching my destination. As I reflected on the source of those feelings, I discovered that somewhere within I thought turning around had undermined my reputation as a mountain man. Once it came into the light, I laughed at the foolishness of the thought. There was ugly pride hidden in there. The moment it was exposed it lost all power and vanished.

All of us tend to operate on default, not paying attention to what's going on under the surface. Unfortunately our underlying tendencies are often not very pretty. We have these animal instincts that drive us if we don't pay attention. We default to a need for control, power, prestige, recognition, etc. The answer isn't to fight these things, but to bring them into the light and see them for what they are. By paying careful attention to our inner world we can find freedom from chains we didn't even know had held us in their grip.

Freedom of the Seasons

It has now been many years since I first started working as a landscape photographer. As a result, I've been able to watch the seasons come and go in a way that few are able to experience. For me it isn't something that happens outside my window, but something more visceral and immersive. Most days I am able to experience nature as it transitions through the year.

Though I have a pretty good idea of what is coming next, I usually struggle with the change. Just as we begin to get the prettiest snows of the year, often in early May, a rainstorm wipes most of it out. As the flowers in the high country reach peak bloom, a frost kills them overnight. Just as the aspen trees begin to glow with golden colors, a windstorm rips them from the trees. All this happens with almost predictable regularity.

I'm slowly coming to accept that there is little in life that I control. Realizing and accepting this is actually freeing. I'm learning that an open hand is better than a clenched fist. Surprisingly, it seems to lead to a more open heart as well. As I learn to walk with open hands, stress loses its grip and my life begins to move toward wholeness. The seasons are slowly teaching me the importance of letting go.

WELL-TENDED GARDEN

After finishing my morning photography, I love to find a big flat rock where I can relax and enjoy the view. Soon the warmth of the day's first rays of sunlight reach me and I begin to unwind. During these times of stillness I sometimes find my mind spinning around something I've done, said, or felt the previous day or week. My thoughts often begin with superficial judgments: It was their fault; I had no other choice; It really wasn't that bad; etc. My tendency is to stop there, but there is always so much more beneath the surface. Some of these thoughts are actually weeds with roots that choke off life from everything around them. It takes some time, a bit of work, and a great deal of vulnerability to uncover those deeply hidden roots and discover their source.

The way we can begin to get to the bottom of our real motivations and feelings is to ask ourselves questions such as: What am I afraid of? Why do I need this? Where did that response come from? The more honest we are, the more clarity and freedom we will gain. Amazingly, when we bring all those hidden thoughts and feelings out into view, they quickly wither and lose their power. And as we continue to address the weeds of our inner world, our outer reactions also change and our lives can grow into the beautiful, flourishing gardens they were always meant to be.

HUMILITY

In the 1600s Galileo Galilei, building on the work of Copernicus, came to the conclusion that the earth revolved around the sun rather than the other way around. This was declared to be heresy, as it undermined the centrality of humanity in creation. However, it eventually became undeniable. In 1859 Charles Darwin published On the Origin of Species, showing again that humans are not at the center, but on the periphery of the chain of life. In the ensuing years our knowledge of the universe has expanded and we've begun to realize that our solar system isn't anywhere near the center of the cosmos. Instead it is an infinitesimally tiny branch of one galaxy among billions of galaxies. Today, scientists are exploring whether there are even other dimensions beyond this one.

Each new discovery forces us to release our sense of self-importance. We once understood the world as revolving around us, but we're learning that not only are we not at the center, we are fragile creatures living on a speck of dust in a far corner of the universe. Such knowledge at first seems crushing. Our utter insignificance is exposed. Our pride, arrogance, and self-importance are all shown to be foolishness. We stand naked before reality and are humbled. It may feel like a tragedy, but perhaps it's what we most need. Our greatest mistakes, our wars, and the damage we've done to this planet and to each other have all stemmed from our sense of self-importance. Perhaps letting go of this and gaining a realistic understanding of our place in the cosmos will help us move toward the way of peace both within and without.

FEAR

When I first moved to Rocky Mountain National Park, I was quite scared on those initial early-morning hikes up to Dream Lake or Mills Lake. I was sure there was a bear or a mountain lion right off the trail just waiting to attack me. Every muscle in my body was tense, adrenaline was coursing through my veins, and I was on high alert. During those early days fear was a close companion and the world around me was like an enemy I had to guard against.

Over the years this foreign and scary place became a friend. I have hiked and skied somewhere between 8,000 and 10,000 miles through the mountains of Rocky Mountain National Park, most of it alone and much of it at night. Now I can't help but laugh at that fear. It came from ignorance and held me captive. It caused me to view the world with tunnel vision and an adversarial perspective.

One of the more important lessons of my life these last years has been realizing how fear tends to blind and imprison us. It makes us do rash and unhealthy things. It is also the prime tool of those who want to manipulate us and is a particularly favorite instrument of politicians. Yes, there is a place for caution and wisdom, but not for fear. Fear keeps us captive and distorts reality. These days when I find I am afraid of something or someone, I know it's time to lean in and look fear in the face. It is the only way to stay free of its grip and to see life as it truly is.

The Oasis

Unspeakable violence, accusations slung back and forth, economic crises, corporate greed, and headlines filled with all manner of ugliness confront us day after day. It probably affects us much more deeply than we realize. Most of us respond by becoming angry with those we feel are to blame. We are certain we know what the real problems are and how to fix them.

Nature refuses to take part in this angry world. It sits apart in stillness and peace as if in tune with a different reality. All the while it gently and quietly calls out to each of us, inviting us to sit in silence beside its still waters. It seems like foolishness to abandon life's clamoring demands to sit in stillness doing what appears to be nothing. Yet that stillness to which nature calls us is far from doing nothing; it is healing our souls. In the silence we begin to see how we too have been caught up in the cycle of hate and blame.

While there is clearly pain and struggle in the natural world, it is honestly shown, without accusation or retribution. At the same time nature openly reveals beauty and goodness. It shows us a way of living with open hands that refuse to grasp and cling or point and blame. This may seem naïve and ineffective, but living differently is the only way we will break the cycle of anger in us and in our society. The flowers and trees, marmots and bees all speak of a different way of living, a way to regain our selves and heal our lives. Step out of the madness and sit in the silence with me. If you listen long enough, you'll hear it too.

The Enemy

In the natural world nearly every animal lives with a watchful eye for their enemy. The deer keep watch for coyote, the bighorn sheep for mountain lions, and the rabbits for bobcats. It is all very clear. But who is our enemy?

Unlike the animal world, our enemy is not somewhere out there ready to pounce. Our enemy is within. It is the voice of fear that causes us to react and retract from others. It is the hate that eats at our heart like a strong acid. It is our need to be right, our need to prove that we have the correct view. The enemy is our arrogance, which is only a mask for our own insecurity. Our enemy is our clenched fist and our tendency to try to control everything. It is our greed and self-centeredness that keep us from acknowledging the rest of our human family and the natural world of which we are a part. It is our lines of division between "us" and "them."

"But what about this or that person?" I hear you say. "The one who would do me harm?" Other human beings are never our true enemy. It is always the darkness within them and within ourselves that we must fight, not by humiliating, attacking, or accusing, but by appealing to the goodness within them. As Martin Luther King Jr. said, "Darkness cannot drive out darkness; only light can do that. Hate cannot drive out hate; only love can do that." This is a hard way, but it is also the only way that will bring about real transformation.

KNOWING

When my wife was a young girl in England she studied French in school. She actually studied it for seven years, learning how to parse every verb, write with fluent grammar, and read any book. On her first trip to France, however, she was completely lost. Although she understood much of what was being said, she wasn't able to engage with it. There was a difference between classroom learning and actual experience; it took several years of living in Paris for her to interact like a native.

Our Western world tends to be focused on one type of knowing: the classroom form. We fill our heads with information and then believe we have true understanding, even though most of the real knowing has never taken place. This leads to presumption and often to totally missing the essence of what we've learned. We have to deeply experience something to truly know it, to move from knowing about to knowing intimately.

Over the years I've come to realize that much of what I thought I knew, I only knew superficially. I had focused so much on knowing about without truly experiencing. I had to let go of my accumulated information and open my heart. Only after engaging on a deeper level could I see how that factual knowledge fit or didn't fit the reality. In order to truly understand anything—from the flowers by the trail to the person sitting next to me—I need to open myself to a deeper form of knowing.

BARK

Drop me anywhere in the middle of the woods and I'll be in my happy place: listening to the birds and the wind singing high above, exploring life on the forest floor, and examining the plants, especially the trees. I find trees to be fascinating and can get lost in them for a long time. The aspen with their smooth slender trunks are often coated in a white powder that some say is a natural sun block. Nearly all the coniferous trees wear a thick armor to protect them from fire and animals. Perhaps the most compelling of them are the old ponderosa with their puzzle-like bark infused with the smell of butterscotch. It has only recently been discovered that, while the trees may have their layers of protection above ground, below the forest floor they intertwine and display a unique interconnectedness, sharing nutrients with one another as each has need.

There are so many people who have developed their own thick bark as a result of being wounded. It is a natural way to try to protect oneself from being hurt again. Humans aren't supposed to have hard crusts like the trees. We are healthiest when we have intimate connections with other people who are able to both encourage and challenge us. There are no guarantees that we won't ever be hurt again, still the rewards of vulnerability (within a healthy community) are worth the risk.

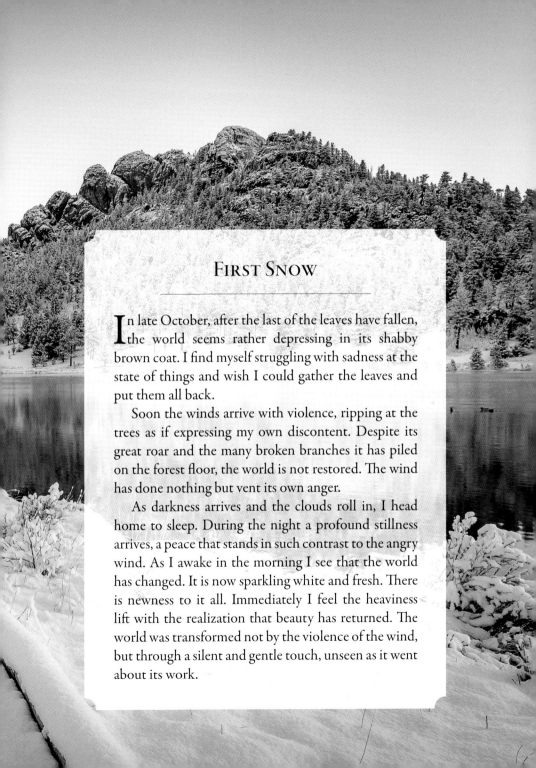

First Snow

In late October, after the last of the leaves have fallen, the world seems rather depressing in its shabby brown coat. I find myself struggling with sadness at the state of things and wish I could gather the leaves and put them all back.

Soon the winds arrive with violence, ripping at the trees as if expressing my own discontent. Despite its great roar and the many broken branches it has piled on the forest floor, the world is not restored. The wind has done nothing but vent its own anger.

As darkness arrives and the clouds roll in, I head home to sleep. During the night a profound stillness arrives, a peace that stands in such contrast to the angry wind. As I awake in the morning I see that the world has changed. It is now sparkling white and fresh. There is newness to it all. Immediately I feel the heaviness lift with the realization that beauty has returned. The world was transformed not by the violence of the wind, but through a silent and gentle touch, unseen as it went about its work.

Evolve

At times people who read my writings on the natural world consider me to be rather naïve or perhaps just ignorant about the reality of nature. My writings are mostly hopeful and focus on seeing the good that is to be found in our wild places, finding examples that can challenge us to live more meaningfully. I certainly understand how one could get the impression that I live with my head in the clouds.

Nature can be a harsh and violent place, where a pack of coyote chase down an injured deer, where eagles snatch rabbits as they go about their daily lives, and where a bear might even feed on its own young. There is much that happens in the wild that seems cruel. Some within our society see the strong taking advantage of the weak as the normal and natural way. It is certainly the way from which we've come. This is our history. This is who we were.

In my mind, one of the main characteristics that makes humans unique is that we have this voice deep within that calls us out from our animal tendencies toward a different way of being. Where selfishness might be the natural thing, we hear a call to compassion and selflessness. Where arrogance might come easily, we hear an internal call to humility and honoring all.

This is the struggle of humanity. Together we wrestle with who we were and who we might become. Each day, we face dozens of choices between the way of the beast and the call of our conscience. From my perspective it seems that we are being called to evolve in the direction of love.

Worth the Effort?

Climbing a mountain is hard work. It normally requires a very early start, sometimes hiking through deep forest in the dark, the crossing of numerous streams, and a grueling push upward through barren rocky terrain. Many people look at this and think it can't possibly be worth the effort. From a distance it looks painful and exhausting. Yet those who reach the summit and experience the elation that comes with it would say otherwise. Most would even say, painful though it was, the journey to the summit was also rewarding in its own way.

Our internal journey toward wholeness is similar, for it requires us to face our inner selves; we often have to walk through the dark forest of our fears and hidden motivations. It involves some hard work as we push through the rocky terrain of our inner life and let go our burdens and addictions. From the outside it looks like it requires too much sacrifice and hardship, but the reality is the opposite. What we find along the way is a lightening of our load. The worries that sapped our strength, the issues we tried to ignore, and the pain that made us limp begin to drop away along the side of the path. Each step gets lighter and a smile begins to grow as we realize we are being freed. We find ourselves sleeping more soundly, recognizing beauty where previously we didn't see any, and loving others as we have always wanted to be loved. We discover we no longer need to try to be someone, for we are already accepted as we are. We sense that we are starting to enter life in all its goodness as we slowly become aware that we are walking into the warm embrace of deep belonging and authentic becoming.

A voice is in the wind I do not know;
A meaning on the face of the high hills
Whose utterance I cannot comprehend.
A something is behind them.

– GEORGE MACDONALD

Internal Breeze

When I sit in a forest and close my eyes, I hear the wind in the treetops high above. At the very same moment I feel something happening inside me. There is a moving and swelling, as if my heart is somehow being blown by a gentle wind.

As I begin to listen more closely I can hear a murmur of indistinct voices within speaking to my heart. Though I don't understand a single word, I can feel a growing sense of joy welling up. What might these voices be saying that makes my heart expand like this? Where do they come from? Are they the secret whispers of the wild, the very heart of creation speaking directly to me? Oh, how I wish I could listen in. Though I don't understand the language it is clear that they speak words of peace, hope, and goodness, for this is plain from the way my heart sings.

BEHIND THE WIND

What is this whisper I hear in the stillness, this voice I hear calling out to my heart when the cares of the world drop away? I hear it call my name; I hear it call me toward goodness, wholeness, and beauty. If you create the space and listen carefully, you will hear it too, for it moves over the whole earth like a gentle breeze. I'm sure you've heard it speak to you before, though you may not have given it the attention it deserves.

I refer to this force, this voice, this movement as God, but you may be more comfortable calling it Mystery, Beauty, Wholeness, Goodness, Purpose, Light, or Love itself. You wouldn't be wrong. As I've pursued this voice I've found it to be all of those and much more. It seems intent on relentlessly pursuing each of us, though ever so gently. It never forces itself upon us and yet waits quietly for us to pay attention. When we finally do begin to listen, it takes us on a wild journey into ourselves and out the other side. It seems intent on leading us into health and wholeness, freeing us from the garbage and wounds we've accumulated on the way.

You may not believe in anything beyond the reach of what you can touch or measure, but it is hard to deny that deep internal whisper. Call it what you will, it seems to know the way. Perhaps you should pursue it and see where it might lead.

UNDERCURRENT

Mountain lakes can at times be a bit deceptive. On windless days they seem to be completely still as they reflect the world around them. The water appears to be at rest in its beautiful setting, but something is happening beneath the surface. There is a gentle undercurrent running from the lake's inlet to the outlet on its far side. It is as if there is a hidden river just under the surface, unnoticed by all but the few who pay very careful attention to its gentle movements.

There seems to be a similar undercurrent running through all of life, though recognized by very few. We're all so busy, rushing from one thing to the next, that we don't take the time to sit and pay attention. As a result we miss much of the deeper work that is happening within. Just as in nature, this gentle current runs downward, away from the towering mountains, away from power, greatness, and renown. Instead it flows towards humility, simplicity, and service.

The flow is so gentle, it is easily overcome. Our tendency is to fight, to gain recognition, to take hold of some form of power or greatness to bring meaning to our lives and overcome our deep and painful insecurity. Yet we are going against the undercurrent that is meant to lead us toward wholeness. Pay attention and follow the gentle current. You will find that it takes you on a journey into meaning, depth, and purpose of which the rest of the world is unaware.

UNDRESS

In a thousand different voices and a million different scenes the world is calling out our names—calling us to undress, to take off our masks of self-assurance and arrogance and become as little children. It is calling us to come and play in the mystery, to encounter the love and beauty that lies behind all things.

Our plastic world subconsciously teaches us from youth to hide our flaws and pretend we are something different than what we know to be true. Beneath the shiny surface of our lives is a murky bottom of pain, failure, and shame. In it we hide both the wrongs we have done and the wrongs committed against us. The pain and the wounds extend deeply below the surface, unseen by all who pass by. We compare what we know to be true of ourselves with the pretty surface of another while they are doing the same to us, perpetuating this false reality.

The quiet whisper we all tend to fear is the call to vulnerability, to openness with ourselves and each other. There is perhaps nothing scarier for a person than to face themselves as they really are. Yet those who are brave enough to step into the light find healing they never knew was possible, unexpected acceptance by others, and a deep sense of wholeness, peace, joy, and hope. This different way to live has been calling out to us from the foundation of the world.

THE WELCOME

We first enter the wilderness as strangers with a sense of unease, unsure of our own safety and a little afraid of the unknown. Yet within a few days of being alone in nature, we begin to realize we are a part of this natural world. It is almost like we are family members returning home. There is still much to learn but we begin to develop a sense of belonging.

Our internal world mirrors this experience, except that this sense of belonging can be much more profound. As we listen to the gentle whisper, we sense we are being welcomed, embraced, and completely loved as we are. There is a feeling of almost limitless peace and joy as we realize we don't need to do anything to receive this embrace. It is simply there waiting. All we have to do is respond to its invitation.

HERALDS OF SPRING

Every spring I stand in awe of the bluebirds. These small colorful birds begin to arrive in early March just as winter in the Rocky Mountains begins to pick up momentum. During the next two months our heaviest snows of the year will arrive, turning the windswept mountains into a world of white.

Yet the bluebirds bring with them a sense of hope. They are like prophets letting us know spring is on its way even though everything around us seems to indicate that winter will never end. They are heralds of spring, proclaiming a reality that has not yet arrived, giving hope to all oppressed by the dark winter days. As they sing their spring songs their message may appear to be foolishness or wishful thinking, but those of us who have lived in the mountains know they speak the truth: that spring is on its way despite outer appearances.

In a world where fear and greed seem to be growing ever stronger, couldn't we be heralds of a different way of being? Perhaps we need to live in such a way that we show there is hope for the future: living generously, caring for the natural world, actively serving our neighbors whether near or distant, and holding our arms open toward those who are different than us.

Would our song be heard? Perhaps only by a few. Maybe if we begin to live like spring has come, the world will eventually realize it too.

ADVENTURE AWAITS

The most exciting journeys are those where we don't have everything all worked out and within our control, where we throw ourselves into the adventure, willing to face whatever may lie ahead. One of my favorite things to do is to find a stream and follow it as far as it leads. Some of my favorite photographs and favorite places in Rocky Mountain National Park have been found that way. I've been led into lush flower-filled valleys I didn't know existed and other times I've found myself tightly clinging to the rocks when I've run into an unexpected cliff. It is through these off-the-beaten-path adventures that I've come to know this park intimately, discovering aspects of it that I never expected. It has also revealed more of who I truly am underneath all my outer layers. Nothing lays us bare like being out of our comfort zone.

Adventure, growth, and a deeper life wait for us all, and no hiking or camping is needed to experience it. While all of us are different, wired with varying preferences, strengths, and interests, we all have hidden depths within us, depths that are largely unexplored. We sense mystery and beauty all around us. We find our hearts yearning after things we can't explain. Instead of simply shrugging it all off, be bold and pursue that mystery. Listen to the gentle movements of your heart and follow them into the hidden depths. It is there you will find what your heart has been longing for since the day you were born.

ADDITIONAL READING

Much of what I wrote in this book was influenced by many authors, old and new, who have spoken into my life over the last decade. If you enjoyed this book, here are a few other authors you might also enjoy.

- GEORGE MACDONALD: A Scottish author and poet from the 1800s whose writings spanned various genres, from fantasy to romance novels but always with an unexpected depth. He wrote over 150 books, but here are a few of my favorites to get you started: *The Curate's Awakening; Lilith; Sir Gibbie; A Book of Strife in the Form of the Diary of an Old Soul; Annals of a Quiet Neighborhood; Unspoken Sermons.*

- JOHN O'DONAHUE: An Irish poet and philosopher who had a deep connection with the land of his native Ireland. His books and poems invite the reader into a much more contemplative approach to life and relationship with the earth. Some of his most loved books are *Beauty: The Invisible Embrace; Anam Čara: A Book of Celtic Wisdom;* and *To Bless the Space Between Us.*

- MARY OLIVER: A distinguished American poet who is able to communicate her connection with nature in a way that it is almost tangible. Check out her books *Why I Wake Early; A Thousand Mornings; The Leaf and the Cloud; etc.*

- RICHARD ROHR: A Franciscan priest and founder of the Center for Action and Contemplation in Albuquerque, New Mexico, with an education in philosophy, psychology, natural sciences, and the spiritual life. He challenges paradigms and presents a new perspective on life and faith. Some of his best books are *Falling Upward; The Naked Now; Simplicity;* and *Everything Belongs.*

- JOHN MUIR: An author and environmental advocate in the late 1800s and early 1900s who did more to preserve the western landscape than almost anyone. His writings show a deep respect and connection with the natural world that is much deeper and more spiritual than most environmental writings of today. Some of his more well-known books are *The Yosemite; Travels in Alaska; Steep Trails;* and *The Mountains of California.*

- THOMAS MERTON: An American Trappist monk and author of over 70 books on the spiritual life. His later works on contemplation are truly challenging: *New Seeds of Contemplation; Thoughts in Solitude;* and *No Man Is an Island.*

About The Author

Erik Stensland was born in Minnesota in 1968 but moved many times before he was 18. His first real memories are from the mountains outside of Helena, Montana, where at ages 5 and 6 he would spend his days hiking through the forest, exploring miles of mountain terrain around his house. Everywhere he moved he was drawn to the natural world, spending his days creating his own secret trails up to the top of nearby hills or climbing a tree to get a better view. His junior high and high school years were spent cycling throughout the countryside where he could enjoy quiet and beautiful views. Throughout Erik's life, the beauty of nature has called to him.

After college Erik moved overseas, living in Austria, Bulgaria, Albania, and Kosovo. He met his wife, Joanna, in Austria and they spent over a decade working with the Albanian people, doing everything from creating an ecotourism program, teaching English, assisting local artists, starting a refugee agency, helping local churches meet the needs of their society, and many other projects.

In 2004 Erik and Joanna moved to Colorado, and Erik took up photography as a way to restore his soul and pay the bills. In 2007 Erik opened his gallery in Estes Park. Since then Erik has become one of the primary photographers focusing on Rocky Mountain National Park. He's published numerous books, opened other gallery and display locations, and contributes to various local and national publications.

Erik's writing and photography are visible expressions of his internal world, which is grounded in a deep Christian faith. It is only during the last decade that he has discovered a spiritual depth he never knew existed, a reality beyond anything he anticipated. His world shifted from a cerebral faith to encountering one who is greater than he could wrap his mind around. Here he discovered untarnished beauty that set him on a fresh journey of discovery and intimacy with God.

ABOUT THE IMAGES

The images in this book were all taken in and around Rocky Mountain National Park in Colorado. If one of these images has spoken to you, you can order it as a fine-art print. They are available in a wide variety of sizes and formats. Call the Images of RMNP gallery in Estes Park, Colorado, at 970-586-4352 for more information or to place an order.

Below I have listed a bit of information about each photo, including titles for those that have them. I have only listed the locations of photos taken from an official trail and have not included the locations of off-trail locations in an effort to help preserve them.

Cover Image: *North Inlet Journey*: A forested trail scene along the North Inlet Trail on the west side of Rocky Mountain National Park.

Page 6: In early October a winter storm moved in, creating an ethereal scene as falling snow and fog turned the forest into a painterly scene.

Page 8: Sunlight breaks through the forest shortly after dawn along the North Inlet on the west side of the park.

Pages 12–13: A winding path makes its way through the forest near Mirror Lake on the northern end of Rocky.

Page 14: *Tarns of Solitude*: This very remote view is one of my favorite places in the park. I sometimes travel here in my thoughts on those days when I long to escape.

Page 17: *Restoration Area*: This photo was taken by Dream Lake on a rainy morning. If you look closely you can see the spider web under the sign, glistening with the morning dew.

Page 18: This is the actual cave I wrote about, taken just as the storm was letting up. I shot it with my cell phone. It is the first phone image I've ever published.

Pages 20–21: This is one of the many remote places I love to escape to, as no more than a handful of people visit this area each year. As the sun began to set, the mountain reflected in the perfectly still tarn.

Pages 22–23: *Hope Awakens*: A spring storm dropped a couple of feet of fresh snow. I had intended to ski to Lake Helene for sunrise, but the deep snow slowed me down and instead I captured the sun rising over the pines just off the trail.

Page 24: *Rocky Mountain Tepee*: Sunrise in the Never Summer Mountains on the western edge of Rocky Mountain National Park as an alpine stream makes its way through a field of wildflowers.

Page 27: Fresh snow and low-lying fog made for a mysterious scene on a small stream not far from Hidden Valley.

Page 28: *Shades of Ponderosa*: I was being filmed for a Casio watch commercial when I saw this view along the Lily Mountain Trail and simply had to stop to photograph the repeating patterns of the ponderosa trunks.

Pages 30–31: *Trail Ridge Sunrise*: The rising sun breaks through the low-lying clouds as seen from above Trail Ridge Road at the start of a beautiful new day.

Page 33: Moonlight illuminates the Never Summer Mountains as seen from the Gore Range Overlook on Trail Ridge Road while a layer of fog floats over Forest Canyon.

Page 34: *Laurel's Tarn*: While backpacking in a remote part of the park, I stumbled upon this scene of bog laurel blooming near a small pond.

Page 37: Forest Canyon filled with clouds during an inversion. The summit of Longs Peak briefly appeared before being swallowed once again by the clouds. This was photographed from near Rock Cut on Trail Ridge Road.

Page 38: October brought the year's first snowstorm, covering the trees around Dream Lake, while a gentle fog hovered over the lake, creating a dreamy feel.

Page 41: While up on Tombstone Ridge I found myself captivated by the ever-changing clouds at sunset. This one lone cloud stood in contrast to the larger clouds around it.

Page 42: At this remote location a variety of stunning flowers bloom for just a couple of days each year.

Page 45: While exploring a little-visited valley on the western side of the park a thunderstorm rolled in and chased me back down into the trees.

Pages 46–47: *Into the Mystery*: Shortly following my mother's unexpected death I went for a walk on the Ute Trail to grieve. Thick clouds moved in and surrounded me as the sun set, creating this dramatic and mysterious scene.

Page 49: While on a long hike on the west side of Rocky Mountain National Park I heard the sound of a waterfall in the distance and followed the sound until I found this delightful scene.

Pages 50–51: A full moon appears from the clouds shortly after sunset.

Pages 52–53: Late at night I photographed this view of the North Inlet Trail on top of Flattop Mountain as the Milky Way shone overhead.

Page 55: The sun makes a brief appearance at sunrise in Wild Basin before being swallowed by the clouds for the rest of the day.

Pages 56–57: *Misty Mountains*: Rocky spires in Forest Canyon are surrounded by clouds on a stormy day, as seen from Trail Ridge Road.

Pages 58–59: The last few leaves of an aspen grove cling to the branches at the end of autumn.

Page 61: *Aspen Trio*: These aspen were photographed on a damp October morning. This photo can be seen in some of the rooms at the Four Seasons Hotel Denver.

Page 62: *Verna's Last Light*: A February sunset at Lake Verna on the west side of Rocky Mountain National Park. It was a long day and night of skiing to get this one.

Pages 64–65: *Spring in the Kawuneeche*: A storm moves in over Baker Mountain in the Kawuneeche Valley on an early June morning.

Pages 66–67: On a stormy morning the rising sun finds a small crack in the clouds and illuminates the tundra.

Page 69: *Sunset High*: After a long hike and climbing several peaks, I reached this view over one of the highest lakes in the park just in time to catch the sun setting over the Never Summer Mountains.

Page 70: Several years after a fire swept through the Cub Lake area I captured a series of photos showing how it is returning back to life.

Pages 72–73: This is one of my favorite trails in Rocky Mountain National Park, the East Inlet Trail that extends seven miles from Grand Lake to Lake Verna. It is a delightfully peaceful hike.

Page 74: Mount Richthofen catches the day's last light on an August evening.

Page 77: *Antler Falls*: While exploring a small stream, I came across this scene. A large elk had died right here beside this little waterfall. The rest of his bones lay nearby.

Page 78: *Dancing Ponderosa*: Ponderosa pines are probably my favorite trees. They seem to have such personality. In the winter their orange trunks contrast so beautifully with the white snow that I am always taking photos of them. This one is near Deer Ridge Junction.

Pages 80–81: In the autumn I normally focus on capturing aspen trees showing off their foliage, but on this walk through a forest I noticed the beauty that was right at my feet.

Page 83: This is the rarely seen southwestern face of Longs Peak as seen from the Wild Basin area.

Page 84: A delightful October morning in an aspen grove near Moraine Park.

Page 87: Autumn along Wild Basin's Campsite Trail.

Page 88: About seven miles back from the nearest trailhead, a large spruce tree catches the warm morning light at the start of a gorgeous new day.

Pages 90–91: On a stormy spring evening on Trail Ridge Road the sun sets behind Mount Richthofen and Specimen Mountain.

Page 93: *Sunrise from the Cliff*: A lone tree clings to the side of a cliff at sunrise on the eastern edge of Rocky Mountain National Park.

Pages 94–95: *Tall Dalmatians*: A stand of aspen covered in scars from the teeth of hungry elk is experiencing the changing seasons.

Page 97: *Columbine Bouquet*: A couple of purple columbine show off their beauty during the month of July in Rocky's backcountry.

Page 98: *Aspen Silence*: A few aspen trees stand quietly during harsh winter conditions near MacGregor Ranch.

Pages 100–101: *Misty Symmetry*: A misty morning in the Kawuneeche Valley near the Beaver Ponds pull-off.

Pages 102–103: *Mountain Light*: As a thunderstorm breaks, the sun lights the pinnacles of a remote mountain on the west side of the park.

Page 104: The Ute Trail stretches out to the west at sunset on an autumn evening.

Page 107: A big boulder of gneiss shows off its many layers as lichen grows around one of its cracks.

Pages 108–109: *Morning Song*: An autumn sunrise makes Notchtop Mountain look as if it is on fire.

Page 110: Clouds swirl around Lumpy Ridge following an autumn storm.

Page 113: Green aspen trees stand in contrast to the fresh snow of a spring storm below Twin Sisters Peaks.

Pages 114–115: *Longing for Light*: A dramatic sunrise lights the sky over Moraine Park.

Page 116: A lone skier makes his way up the mountain in Hidden Valley.

Pages 118–119: *Morning Surprise*: A field of wildflowers celebrates the start of a new day near tree line.

Page 120: *Klimt's Aspen*: An aspen tree shows a bit of flair at the peak of its autumn colors.

Pages 122–123: Pinecones on a ponderosa tree open up with the arrival of winter.

Page 125: *Northern Pinnacle*: An unnamed peak reflects in Mirror Lake on the northern border of Rocky.

Page 126: *Adoration*: Flowers abound in this high meadow at sunrise in early August.

Pages 128–129: *The Smile of Summer*: During an amazing summer bloom, alpine sunflowers seem to fill the tundra.

Page 130: *Silent Light*: A billion suns fill the sky above Lake Irene just off of Trail Ridge Road.

Page 133: *Peeking Through*: Longs Peak is briefly visible through the clouds on a spring morning.

Page 134: *Triple Falls*: This remote set of waterfalls, far off the beaten path, is as pretty as can be.

Pages 136–137: A bull elk stands silhouetted at sunset on the tundra. It is the time of year when the velvet on their antlers shed.

Page 138: Alpine sunflowers and one small forget-me-not bloom beside a lichen-covered boulder in the tundra.

Page 141: The rough bark of a ponderosa pine tree on the eastern edge of Horseshoe Park reminds me of some sort of natural puzzle.

Pages 142–143: The spring had already arrived and melted all the snow when we received a surprise May snowfall that covered the area around Lily Lake in a fresh white coat.

Page 145: *Trail to Infinity*: The Milky Way fills the sky above the trail near Lake Irene.

Pages 146–147: McHenry's Peak reflects in a tarn at sunrise in Glacier Gorge.

Pages 148–149: While finishing this book, I experienced this amazing sunset over the Never Summer Mountains and knew I needed to include it.

Page 151: *Western Summer*: The Never Summer Mountains glow at sunrise on the west side of Rocky Mountain National Park.

Page 152: *Alluvial Sunburst*: The sun breaks through the trees on an autumn morning at the Alluvial Fan.

Page 155: *Stormy Pinnacles*: While camping in an out-of-the-way area, a storm moved in at sunset, creating a gentle but strangely colored sunset over this jagged peak.

Page 156: *Pools of Hope*: A series of unusually shaped tarns reflect the sky in an isolated valley of Rocky.

Pages 158–159: At tree line a lone tarn sits in stillness on a late-August afternoon.

Page 161: *Herald of Spring*: A bluebird arrives in early spring, letting us know that summer is coming soon. This one was near the Beaver Meadows entrance to Rocky Mountain National Park.

Pages 162–163: Mummy Mountain catches the last light of the day as a stream rushes downhill toward Lawn Lake.

Pages 166: Erik sits under the shelter of an overhanging rock during a rain storm on the Lake Nanita trail in June 2017 while working on this book.

ALSO BY ERIK STENSLAND

- *Wild Light: A Celebration of Rocky Mountain National Park*

- *Memories of Rocky Mountain National Park*

- *The Landscape Photographer's Guide: Photographing Rocky Mountain National Park*

- Rocky Mountain National Park yearly calendars

- Blu-ray: *Into the Wonder*

These and many other products by Erik Stensland can be found on the Images of Rocky Mountain National Park website:

www.ImagesofRMNP.com.

GALLERY

If you visit Estes Park, Colorado, make sure to stop by the Images of RMNP gallery. Here you will find a large number of fine-art photographs on display as well as books, cards, calendars, and much more. Erik also has other gallery locations that you can learn about on our website.

Images of RMNP is located at
203 Park Lane, Estes Park, Colorado.

We are online at: ImagesofRMNP.com. Erik also posts daily on his *Erik Stensland Fine Art Photography* Facebook page and on Twitter @ErikthePhotog. The Images of RMNP gallery also posts regularly on Facebook and Instagram.